Deepwater Disaster

SEABIRD RESCUE!

BY JAMES BUCKLEY JR.

ILLUSTRATED BY KERSTIN LACROSS

BEARPORT
PUBLISHING

Minneapolis, Minnesota

BEAR CLAW

Credits

Interior coloring by Jon Siruno.
Photos: 22T © AP Photos; 22B © Jon Hrusa/IFAW/AP Photos.

Bearport Publishing
Minneapolis, MN
President: Jen Jenson
Director of Product Development: Spencer Brinker
Editor: Allison Juda

Produced by Shoreline Publishing Group LLC
Santa Barbara, California
Designer: Patty Kelley
Editorial Director: James Buckley Jr.

Library of Congress Cataloging-in-Publication Data

Names: Buckley, James, Jr., 1963– author. | LaCross, Kerstin, 1988–
   illustrator.
Title: Deepwater disaster : seabird rescue! / by James Buckley, Jr. ;
   illustrated by Kerstin LaCross.
Description: Bear claw books. | Minneapolis, Minnesota : Bearport
   Publishing Company, [2021] | Series: Rescued! animal escapes | Includes
   bibliographical references and index.
Identifiers: LCCN 2020030846 (print) | LCCN 2020030847 (ebook) | ISBN
   9781647476175 (library binding) | ISBN 9781647476243 (paperback) | ISBN
   9781647476311 (ebook)
Subjects: LCSH: Animal rescue—Juvenile literature. | Wildlife
   rescue—Juvenile literature. | Animals—Effect of oil spills
   on—Juvenile literature. | Oil spills—Juvenile literature.
Classification: LCC HV4708 .B84 2021 (print) | LCC HV4708 (ebook) | DDC
   363.738/20916364—dc23
LC record available at https://lccn.loc.gov/2020030846
LC ebook record available at https://lccn.loc.gov/2020030847

For more information, write to Bearport Publishing, 5357 Penn Avenue South, Minneapolis, MN 55419.
Printed in the United States of America.

Contents

CHAPTER 1

Oil Spills

It's used to make our cars and planes go.

It helps us create light and heat for our homes.

And it is often in the products that we use every day.

What is it?

It's oil! Oil is a big part of everyday life.

Oil comes from deep inside Earth. Huge drills are used to remove it.

Tanker ships, trucks, and pipelines carry the oil where it needs to go. Millions of **barrels** of oil are moved every day.

Most of them arrive safely. But sometimes they don't.

When there's an oil spill or a leak, people, animals, and the environment suffer. Then, it's up the experts to save the day!

CHAPTER 2

Disaster in the Gulf

The Deepwater Horizon drilling platform pumped oil off the coast of Louisiana. The **rig** was surrounded by the warm waters of the Gulf of Mexico.

The drilling rig's pipes reached deep down to the **seabed**. Then, the pipes drilled into the earth until they reached oil and natural gas, another underground product.

PLATFORM

OIL TANKER

5,000 FEET
(1,524 M)

PIPE

The oil traveled through pipes to the platform on the surface.

DRILL

SEABED

OIL

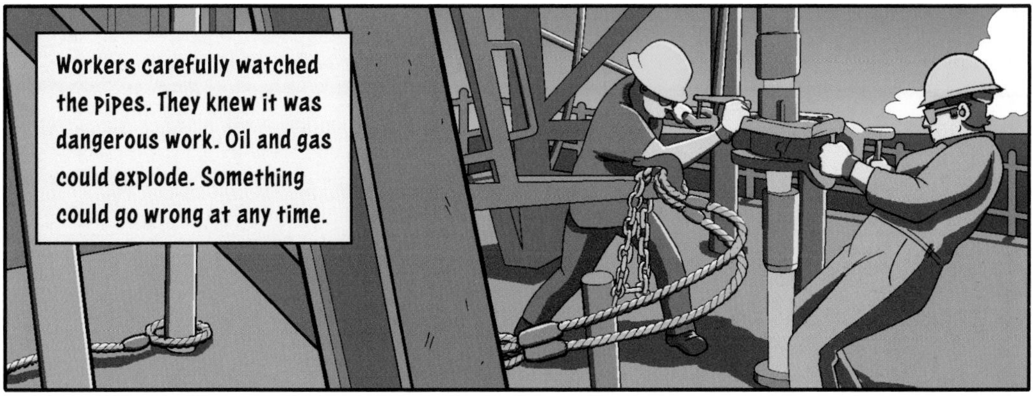
Workers carefully watched the pipes. They knew it was dangerous work. Oil and gas could explode. Something could go wrong at any time.

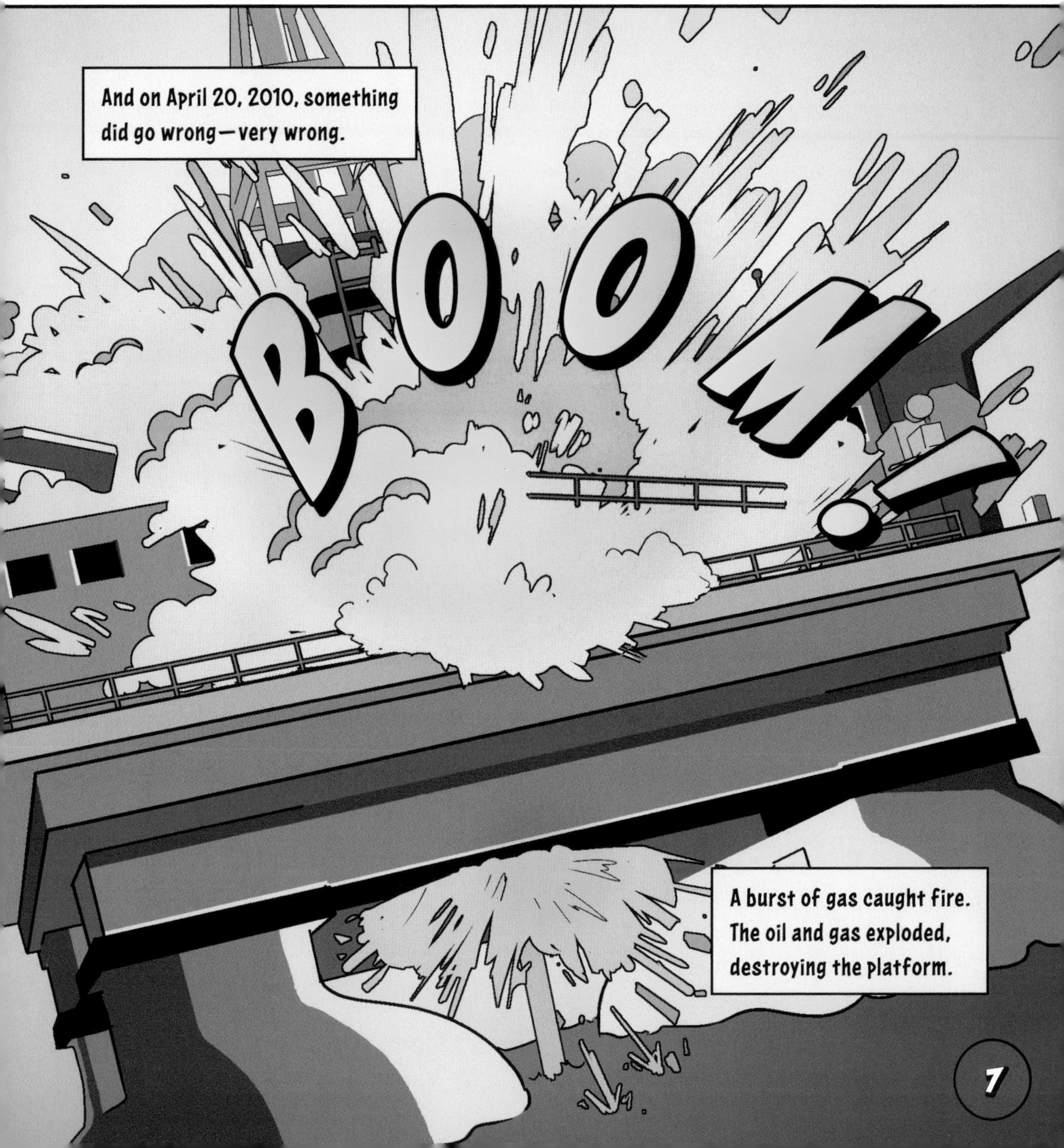
And on April 20, 2010, something did go wrong—very wrong.
BOOM!
A burst of gas caught fire. The oil and gas exploded, destroying the platform.

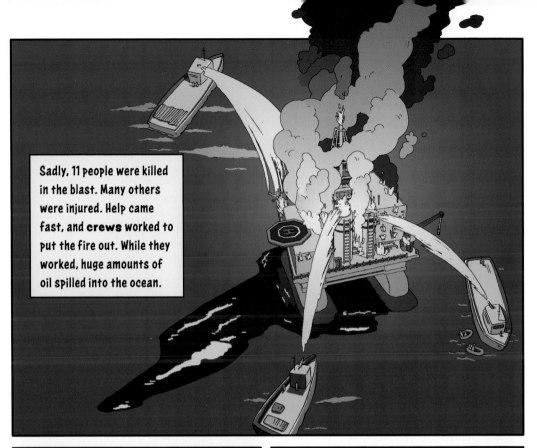

Sadly, 11 people were killed in the blast. Many others were injured. Help came fast, and **crews** worked to put the fire out. While they worked, huge amounts of oil spilled into the ocean.

Rescuers helped the **survivors**, but they knew there was still more work to do.

Millions of gallons of oil poured into the water, endangering all the animals that lived there.

MISSISSIPPI

LOUISIANA

★
Baton
Rouge

Gulf of Mexico

OIL

DEEPWATER HORIZON →

Many sea mammals, such as dolphins, seals, and whales did not survive the spreading oil.

Thousands of sea turtles were also hurt or killed by the growing disaster.

Huge numbers of fish died when they could not breathe in the oily water.

Many **species** of birds lived near the site of the explosion. Sadly, thousands were soon covered with oil.

Birds that flew away from the explosion got covered in oil when they landed back in the water.

Oil was everywhere!

All along the shore, thousands of birds were caught up in the sticky mess.

The brown pelican was facing trouble even before the explosion.

Scientists were trying to save these **endangered** seabirds.

But because of the oil spill, the brown pelican would be in more danger than ever.

The pelicans were in trouble... but help was on the way!

CHAPTER 3

Kayla to the Rescue!

KAYLA, RIGHT?

THAT'S RIGHT.

I'M WITH THE U.S. FISH AND **WILDLIFE** SERVICE.

I'M GLAD YOU'RE HERE. WE REALLY NEED YOUR HELP.

OF COURSE. WE NEED TO WORK TOGETHER TO HELP THESE PELICANS.

WHAT WILL HAPPEN TO THE BIRDS THAT GOT INTO THE OIL?

WILL IT KILL THEM?

IT MIGHT. BUT IF WE GET THERE IN TIME, WE CAN SAVE SOME.

THE OIL DESTROYS THE **WATERPROOF** COATING ON THE PELICANS' FEATHERS.

WITHOUT THIS COATING, THEY CAN FREEZE TO DEATH OR EVEN DROWN.

BUT IF WE CAN CLEAN THEM UP, SOME OF THE BIRDS CAN SAFELY RETURN TO THE WILD.

LOOK!

OVER THERE! HEAD FOR THAT BEACH!

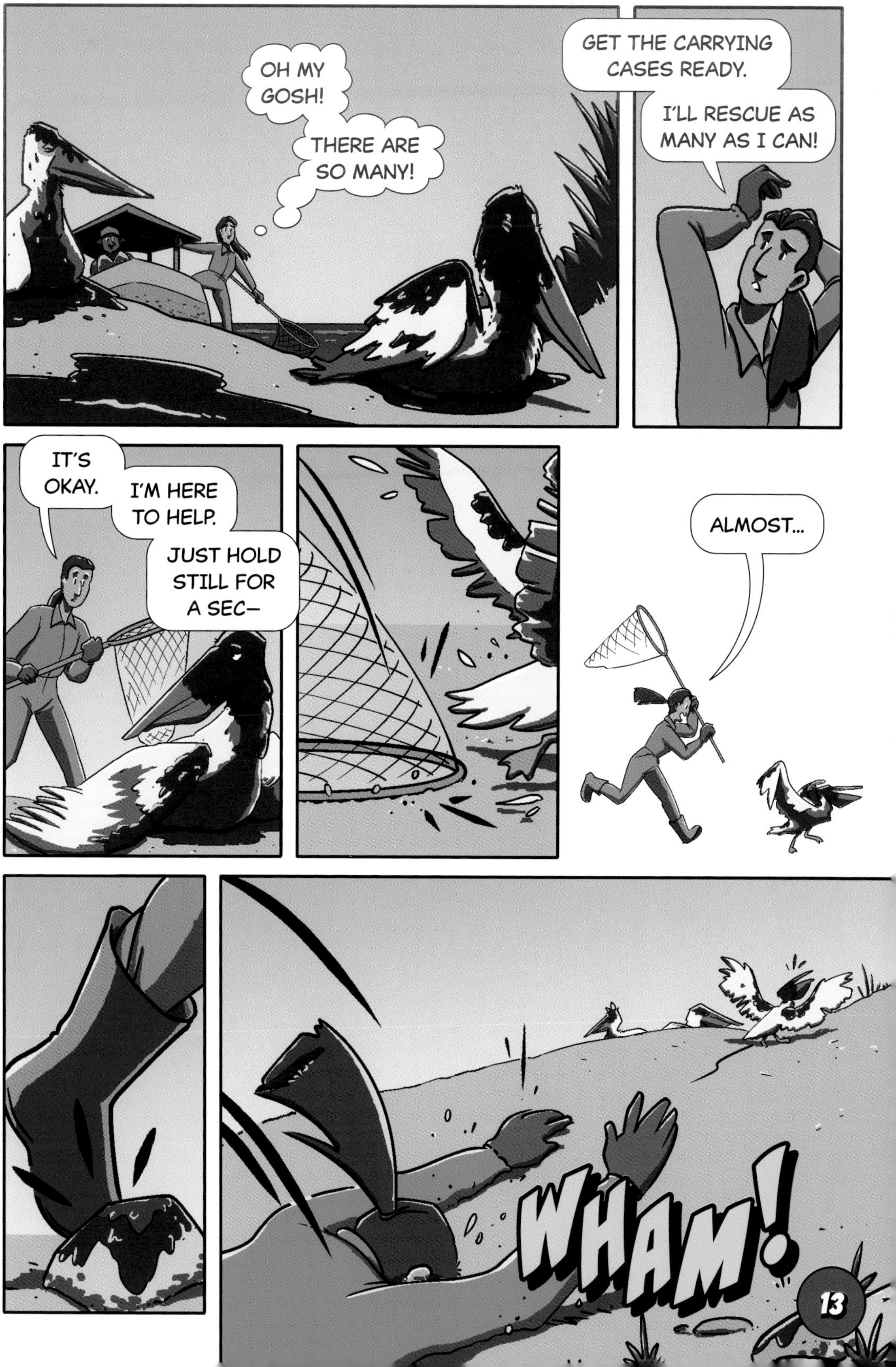

OH MY GOSH!
THERE ARE SO MANY!
GET THE CARRYING CASES READY.
I'LL RESCUE AS MANY AS I CAN!
IT'S OKAY.
I'M HERE TO HELP.
JUST HOLD STILL FOR A SEC—
ALMOST...
WHAM!

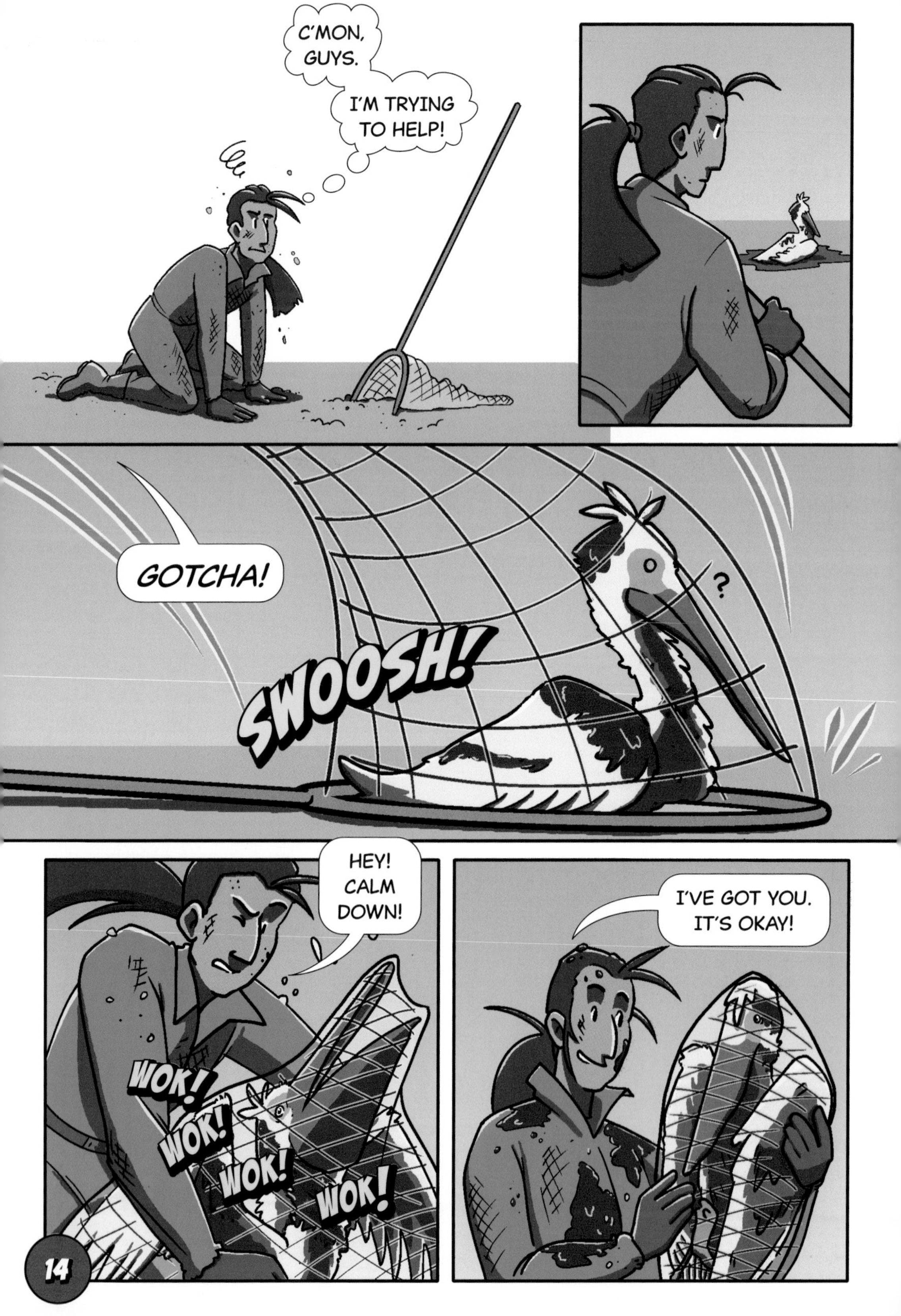
C'MON, GUYS.
I'M TRYING TO HELP!
GOTCHA!
SWOOSH!
?
HEY! CALM DOWN!
WOK!
WOK!
WOK!
WOK!
I'VE GOT YOU. IT'S OKAY!

ONE DOWN, LOTS MORE TO GO!

Kayla gathered as many oily birds as she could.

It was a race against time!

Rescuers also worked fast to save sea turtles that were covered in oil.

The oil could damage the turtles' eyes and lungs.

Sea turtle eggs were also at risk. Eggs can't hatch in oil! Scientists saved some by moving them to a safer place.

They needed to go to parts of the gulf that weren't impacted by the spill.

Weeks later, the eggs could hatch. The baby sea turtles would crawl to the clean water.

With her boat full of birds, Kayla headed to the rescue center.

Kayla joined other rescuers who brought hundreds of birds to cleaning centers.

SEABIRD RECOVERY CENTER

At the centers, the hard, messy work continued.

CHAPTER 4
Cleanup Time

OKAY, WE'VE GOT HER.

HERE'S ANOTHER BROWN PELICAN.

THIS ONE MADE ME CHASE HER!

LET'S GET HER TO THE WASHING STATION.

Workers used special soap to break up the oil. They had to carefully clean every one of the birds' feathers.

Cleaning each bird could take hours.

Then, the birds were rinsed off.

Warm, clean water removed soap and any remaining oil.

Drying the birds took a lot of time. Hot air from dryers helped, but the birds did a lot of the work themselves.

They used their beaks to **preen**, or arrange, their feathers.

The rescue staff made sure the birds had enough to eat while they recovered.

HEY! YOU CLEAN UP PRETTY WELL!

The birds were kept safe at the rescue center while they recovered.

A net-covered tank kept them from flying away too soon!

Another center cleaned the oil-covered sea turtles.

ALMOST DONE!

WE'LL GET YOU BACK TO THE GULF REALLY SOON!

More than 300 turtles were saved by expert animal cleaners.

When the animals were ready, they were released back into the ocean.

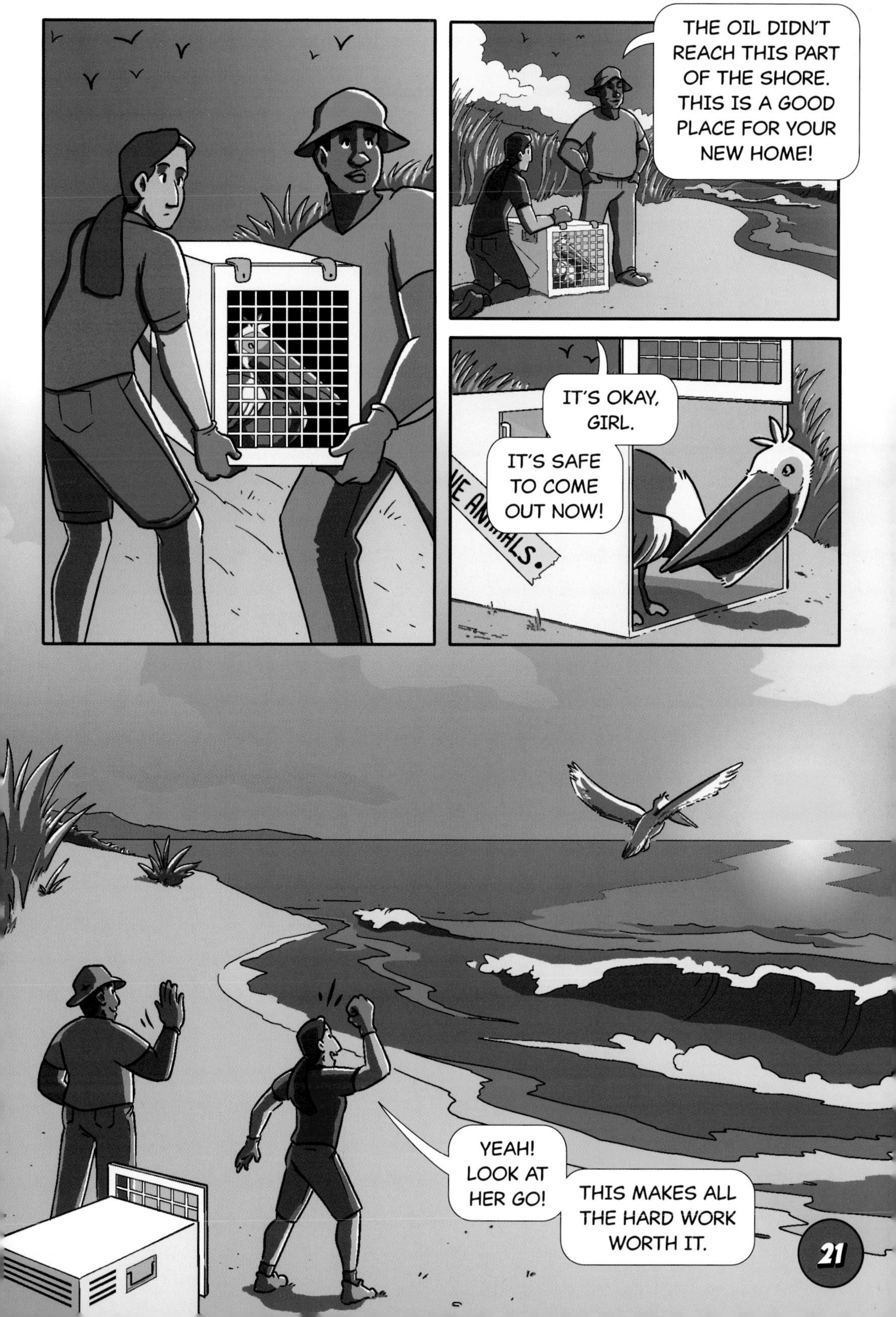
THE OIL DIDN'T REACH THIS PART OF THE SHORE. THIS IS A GOOD PLACE FOR YOUR NEW HOME!
IT'S OKAY, GIRL.
IT'S SAFE TO COME OUT NOW!
YEAH! LOOK AT HER GO!
THIS MAKES ALL THE HARD WORK WORTH IT.

OTHER
TERRIBLE OIL SPILLS

TREASURE SPILL, SOUTH AFRICA

On June 23, 2000, the oil ship *Treasure* sank and spilled about 1,300 tons (1,179 MT) of oil. One of the world's largest populations of African penguins lived on islands near the spill. As oil filled the water, more than 20,000 penguins became covered with oil. Experts from the International Bird Rescue Research Center teamed up with local rescue workers to help the birds. At the time, it was the largest seabird rescue in history.

EXXON VALDEZ SPILL, ALASKA

On October 24, 1989, the *Exxon Valdez* ran into some undersea rocks. The ship spilled about 11 million gallons (42 million L) of oil into Prince William Sound. Hundreds of thousands of animals were covered in oil, but soon help arrived. The International Bird Rescue organization saved more than 1,600 birds. Workers from Friends of the Sea Otter and other groups helped clean more than 300 oily otters.

GLOSSARY

barrels a measurement used for oil; each barrel is about 42 gallons (159 L)

crews groups of people doing the same job

endangered heading toward becoming extinct, or disappearing from Earth

preen to clean or polish

rig an oil platform or oil drilling site

seabed the land at the bottom of the ocean

species groups that animals are divided into, according to similar characteristics

survivors people or animals who are alive following a disaster or accident

waterproof able to prevent water from passing through

wildlife animals that live in the wild

INDEX

READ MORE

Adams, Kenneth. *Oil Drilling and Fracking.* Minneapolis: PowerKids Press, 2019.

Bethea, Nikole Brooks. *Deepwater Horizon (Man-Made Disasters).* Minneapolis: Jump!, 2018.

Sherman, Jill. *Oil Rig Workers (Getting the Job Done).* Minneapolis: PowerKids Press, 2019.

LEARN MORE ONLINE

1. Go to **www.factsurfer.com**
2. Enter "**Deepwater Disaster**" into the search box.
3. Click on the cover of this book to see a list of websites.